Ireland Travel Guide 2023 - 2024

Top 50 Things To Know Before You Go

Clara R. Burgher

Table Of Contents

INTRODUCTION

Welcome to the enchanting world of Ireland, a land where history dances with myth, and landscapes paint a picture of breathtaking beauty. This travel guide, "Ireland Travel Guide 2023-2024," is your passport to unlocking the treasures that this captivating island has to offer. Whether you're an intrepid explorer, a culture enthusiast, or simply seeking an unforgettable escape, this guide is tailored to ensure that your journey through Ireland is as enriching as it is enjoyable. As someone who has personally traversed the emerald hills, explored the ancient ruins, and savored the warmth of Irish hospitality, I'm thrilled to be your guide on this remarkable adventure. Picture yourself strolling down cobblestone streets, sipping a pint of creamy Guinness in a traditional pub, or standing atop rugged cliffs that kiss the Atlantic Ocean. These are the moments that await you, and this guide is designed to make every step of your voyage seamless and memorable. But let me take you back to a misty morning in Connemara, where I first felt the allure of Ireland's magic. The air was crisp, and as I wandered through the verdant countryside, I encountered a local storyteller sharing the tales of ancient Celtic legends. In that moment, surrounded by the embrace of history and nature, I realized that Ireland is not just a destination; it's a tapestry of experiences woven by generations of inhabitants. This travel guide isn't just a collection of facts and figures; it's an invitation to immerse yourself in the heart and soul of Ireland. Each chapter will lead you through essential information, revealing the nuances of weather and climate, the lyrical cadence of the language, the rhythms of daily life, and the iconic places that beckon travelers from around the globe. We'll explore the vibrant cities and quaint villages, sample traditional cuisines that tell stories of a resilient culture, and uncover hidden gems that will leave an indelible mark on your memory. Throughout this journey, you'll find practical insights and insider tips, empowering you to navigate with confidence and make the most of your time in Ireland. Whether you're planning a whirlwind tour or a leisurely escape, the itineraries and day trip suggestions will help you craft an experience that aligns with your interests and desires.

In the pages that follow, we'll embark on a captivating exploration of Ireland's landscapes, culture, and people. Together, we'll discover the top 50 things you need to know before you go, from cultural customs to practical considerations. Additionally, we'll delve into the top 20 things that Ireland is famous for, showcasing the nation's rich history, literary heritage, and remarkable contributions to the world, So, my fellow traveler, let's set forth on this incredible journey. As you turn the pages and absorb the wisdom within, may you find inspiration, joy, and a deeper connection to the heart of Ireland. Your adventure begins here, and I'm honored to be your guide through the pages of "Ireland Travel Guide 2023-2024."

50 THINGS TO KNOW BEFORE YOU GO TO IRELANDS & THE LOCALS

General Info

#1 The North Atlantic, west of Great Britain, contains the island of Ireland. They make up the British Isles together with all the smaller islands.

#2 Politically, the island is split between Northern Ireland, which makes up the remaining third of the island, and the Republic of Ireland, which occupies the southernmost 5/6 of the island. Because Northern Ireland approximately corresponds to Ireland's Ulster area, it is often referred to as Ulster.

#3 Catholics make up the majority of the population in the Republic of Ireland, whilst Protestants make up the majority of the population in Northern Ireland (41.5%). Due to this, Ireland saw a particularly turbulent 20th century that saw civil wars, terrorist assaults, and the deaths of a great number of people.
The tension between Catholics and Protestants has permeated almost every aspect of Irish history, and if you look closely, you can still see it, although more or less hidden.

#4 Things are now considerably more peaceful in Northern Ireland, and it is completely safe to visit there. There are still street art pieces and monuments that serve as reminders of bygone eras, but that is all. This is especially clear in Derry, where we may visit the Bogside Bloody Sunday Memorial and the Free Derry Corner.

#5 There are 6.5 million fewer people living in Ireland now than there were in 1841 (8M). Among developed countries, this is exceedingly rare, if not unique. What happened, then?
The potato harvest failed between 1845 and 1849 as a result of a late blight that destroyed the plant's edible roots and leaves. Ireland's reliance on potatoes was so great that more than 1 million people perished from famine and illness and up to 1.5 million moved, mostly to the US.
The Irish Potato Famine or the Great Famine are common names for this.

Weather & Climate

#6. How would you rate Ireland's weather? Although the temperature is significantly higher than one would think for such a northern country due to the mild North Atlantic current, it rains... a lot (between 150 and 220 days a year).

Due to the Atlantic's significant influence, Ireland seldom experiences severe heat or cold, with temperatures rarely falling below -20 or rising over 300. Ireland typically has chilly summers and warm, rainy winters.

How do you interpret this as a traveler? Summer is a lot better time to travel than winter. Warmer and less rain is falling. But now that everyone is aware of it, everything is much more congested.

#7 In addition, you should take into account how much shorter the days are in the winter, which makes travel more challenging.

When is the ideal time to visit Ireland, then? May, in our opinion, is the ideal month to visit Ireland! There is a lot of sunshine and daylight, there isn't as much rain as there is in the winter, and there aren't yet the massive hordes of visitors.

Language

#8 Irish and English are both official languages in Ireland. Although Irish is regarded as the first and national language, only roughly one-third of the people are able to speak it; in contrast, English is widely spoken.

Keep in mind that Irish people have a strong accent, often to the point of being difficult to understand. Nevertheless, as you get used to it, it becomes simpler.

#9 The Irish are highly outspoken people. It's quite usual to go into a bar and have conversations with other patrons. They stand apart from other individuals in North Europe in this way.

Lifestyle

#10 The smiles and overall friendliness of the Irish will also come as a surprise to you. People will grin at you everywhere—on the streets, in the shops. It greatly simplifies and improves everything. We adored Irish people!

#11 The Irish are famed for having redheadedness. In actuality, the Republic of Ireland has the highest proportion of redheads per capita in the whole globe. However, barely 10% of Irish people are red-headed.

Ireland is a fantastic destination if you like redheads! Just remember not to expect everyone to have red headed.

#12 Ireland is known as the Emerald Island, as you are surely aware. And it's really simple to see why! The whole island is covered with lush, mostly grassland, and flora. That amazing green is the result of all the rain, mild temperatures, and moist air we spoke about before

Where To Visit

#13. There are only three UNESCO World Heritage Sites in Ireland (the island), two of which are in the Republic of Ireland and one in Northern Ireland.

These include

- Northern Ireland's Giant's Causeway and Causeway Coast;
- The Boyne Valley Tombs (commonly known as Newgrange);
- The Skellig Michael Monastery;

Tours, City Views In The Republic of Ireland

#14 When traveling to Ireland, one should be aware that Dublin (and maybe Cork) is quite different from the rest of the country. While Dublin is a contemporary, fast-paced metropolis, Ireland is mostly rural, with many tiny towns and villages moving at a relatively sluggish pace.

#15 Dublin is most vibrant at night when both residents and visitors alike pack the town's bars. One of the things you absolutely must do in Ireland visits a pub and take in the atmosphere.
Go if you can on a night of a rugby or football match; everything will be much more fun.

#16 In addition to its vibrant nightlife, Dublin is home to numerous additional attractions. To rapidly acquire a feel for the city, I highly recommend taking one of the many walking tours. The free walking tour offered by the Sandman was enjoyable and instructive. one of our greatest projects to date. (Nearly on par with Munich's).

PS: You'll probably be permitted to grab boobs at the conclusion of the tour. Upon reflection, this was far superior to Munich.

Travel advice: Do not miss the Trinity College Library or the Book of Kells. One of Ireland's most well-known sights, it.

#17 Founded in the 16th century, the Trinity College Library serves as a legitimate depository for Irish-published publications. One of the most magnificent libraries in the world is undoubtedly The Long Room. We are undoubtedly at our most attractive ever!

The four New Testament Gospels are included in the illuminated manuscript book known as the Book of Kells, which is written in Latin. They are said to be the oldest books in existence and the best national treasures of Ireland, having been created about 800 AD. You must visit there if you are in Dublin!

If you purchase a ticket for the Book of Kells online, you may avoid the lineups and ensure your time slot.

#18 Along with visiting the Trinity College Library, other well-liked activities in Dublin include seeing the Kilmainham Gaol and the Guinness Storehouse.

#19 Let's now leave Dublin and go specifically to Galway. Galway is a lovely seaside city with a rich history. In all honesty, I don't believe the city has anything special, but Galway County offers plenty of intriguing things to do! However, it's worthwhile to wander aimlessly for a while, especially at night.
Make sure to stroll around the Latin Quarter, Quay Street, Shop Street, and Eire Square if you want to do this. Additionally, we highly suggest you visit the waterfront to take in the scenery.
The major reason Galway is so well-liked by tourists is that it makes a great base for seeing the cliffs of Moher, the Burren, Connemara, and the Aran Islands.

#20 The Cliffs of Moher are one of Ireland's top tourist attractions for us. They are stunning in every way. Incredible natural lookouts where you may take in the scenery are created by the curvature of the shoreline and the way the island abruptly ends in a 300-meter-high cliff. Take two or three hours for a hike to the several pathways to the north and south of the official lookouts if you want to really appreciate this location.

You should be aware that there is a parking cost of 8 Euros (per person, not per vehicle) to enter, and it is very difficult to park anywhere other than in the designated parking lot. Sad to see such a natural area enclosed merely to collect a few euros.

Travel tip: You can see the Cliffs, the Burren, and Galway in one day from Dublin, but i highly advise against it unless it's your only choice. You'll get very little enjoyment out of it, and it's very long and exhausting!

#21 The Ring of Kerry is a circular road that circles the Kerry peninsula and is renowned for its bucolic and dramatic views. You should set out a whole day for it since it is highly worthwhile. It's longer than it seems, so allow at least a full day if you want to take your time to stop and really appreciate it.

The Ring of Kerry is now highly well-known among tourists, so you should be prepared for a lot of visitors during the busy season. Consider taking a look at the Dingle peninsula below if this troubles you.

Going in the winter is a possibility, but the climate in this area is quite arid, and you'll probably only experience rain and fog (sadly, we know what we're talking about).

#22 The gorgeous Killarney National Park is located on the border of the Ring and has breathtaking viewpoints like the Ladies' Views, a magnificent waterfall, and a few historical sites including Ross Castle, Muckross Abbey, House, and Gardens.

You should definitely examine the Dunloe Pass in this area, which is just outside the park. It is a lovely, winding mountain route with some of Ireland's most breathtaking scenery. When it rains, there are waterfalls on both sides of the road and watercourses originating from all directions.

#23 When compared to Kerry, the Dingle peninsula has fewer visitors, thus it can be a good alternative if you want to avoid the large crowds. Just keep in mind that it isn't as lovely as Kerry, which is why there are fewer people there.

I advise you to check out the quaint town of Dingle, the breathtaking Slea Head Drive, and the Connor Pass on the Dingle peninsula.

#24 Lastly, there are castles. They're dispersed around Ireland, most of them in ruins. You should be aware that some are overvalued and downright unimpressive. Especially if you come from one of the other European nations with really magnificent castles and palaces.

Nevertheless, some are intriguing and well of a visit, albeit being quite pricey. Our top picks include

- **Blarney Castle,** where you may kiss the Blarney stone backward and get the gift of gab. Keep in mind that admission to the castle and grounds costs 18E.

- The Butler family previously had great authority, and their residence was **Kilkenny Castle**. This exceptionally well-preserved castle offers an engaging guided tour. The guided tour is included in the 8 euro entry price.

- **The Rock of Cashel** is a collection of ancient structures built on a rock, not quite a castle. It's a great cool place to see and a fantastic sight from a distance. It costs 8 euros for the ticket, which also includes a guided tour.

Tours, Best views In Northern Ireland

#25 Northern Ireland's capital and largest city is Belfast. It's a pretty modern city with some historical markers from the past. The Albert

Memorial clock, Belfast Castle, and city hall are perhaps the three most well-known of them.

However, the Titanic Museum in Belfast's revitalized Titanic Quarter is the city's top tourist destination. The whole region seems to be lovely and pleasant to explore. We can't speak for (or against) the museum since we haven't really been there. But the cost is high!

The breakfast baps (see below for more information) and Irish fudge are two of the excellent handmade foods you can get at St. George's Market, which is our favorite place to visit in Belfast.

#26 Derry (or Londonderry, if you're English) is a much smaller town despite being the second-largest city in Northern Ireland. Derry, which is quite near the "border," suffered much throughout the violent 20th century. Bloody Sunday is an illustration of those challenging times.

Derry's walls, which are the finest maintained in Ireland and Great Britain, are its most significant feature. You can walk on them all around, which makes for some pretty beautiful locations. They are extremely remarkable.

The Guildhall is located between the walls and the riverbank. This is an interesting structure that seems to be a church but is really a city hall. Free entry is offered.

#27 The Giant's Causeway, which sits on the north shore of the island, is a unique location and a geological marvel due to its very distinctive rock formations. These recognizable hexagonal volcanic stone formations cover the whole coastline and cliffs. We found this to be a touch unimpressive despite its singularity and unusual structure.

It should be noted that using the visitor's center, which costs a fee, is not required. In other words, if you can park your vehicle, you may visit this UNESCO site for nothing.

#28 The Carrick-a-Rede Rope Bridge, which links the mainland to a resemblance of an island that salmon fishermen initially constructed years ago for salmon fishing, is quite near to the giant's causeway.

While the walk to the bridge is free, crossing it costs quite a bit (8 euros). The little bridge is almost a rope bridge, so you should be aware that there isn't much to see on the opposite side.

However, I still urge you to take action. It's enjoyable and sometimes windy. Anyhow, those 30 seconds were rather pricey.

Many of the locations featured in Game of Thrones were shot in Northern Ireland, as you presumably already know if you're a fan of the series. There are even a few Game of Thrones excursions that enable you to enjoy the whole experience, seeing various locations and even engaging in some role-playing.

Food & Drink

#29 Ireland is not known for its excellent cuisine, and it is hardly a haven for foodies. Nobody travels to Ireland to eat (or drink, maybe). Even so, it's worthwhile to sample a few regional delicacies.

You should be aware that you'll probably have to eat potatoes while you're in Ireland. The Irish prepared potatoes in a variety of ways and used them on everything.

#30 Start with breakfast, which is where we should begin. An English breakfast is comparable to a full Irish breakfast. One of the few recipes that most likely won't include potatoes is this one.

The most often used components are bacon rashers, pig sausages, fried or scrambled eggs, white or black pudding, bread, and fried tomatoes, although sometimes beans and mushrooms may also be included. So, little things

#31 Compared to a regular breakfast, the morning bap or roll is superior. The complete Irish breakfast has been modified for the contemporary, mobile age. It has practically all of the components of a typical full Irish breakfast but in soft bread (the bap). It tastes and looks just as good!

St. George's Market in Belfast is the finest location we are aware of to consume these bombs!

#32 Irish butter is yet another well-known Irish foodstuff. To be honest, I couldn't really tell the difference at first, but after doing some research, I found out that "Irish butter is a European-style butter and compared to typical American butter, it has more butterfat".

The butter will have a richer, creamier texture as a result. Our favorite Irish butter brand is Kerrygold, which differs somewhat from other European/Irish butter products in that it has a lot more taste.

#33 The Boxty is a classic Irish potato pancake that combines shredded and mashed potatoes for a texture that is halfway between a pancake and a hash brown. In all honesty, I had hoped for it to be much better; it's decent, but not spectacular.

#34 The seafood chowder is another popular Irish ritual. The typical components include fish (such as salmon, cod, etc.) and shellfish, together with potatoes, onions, celery, corn, carrots, bacon, and cream.

Although we had very high hopes for this, it fell short. The cream masks the fish's taste. We didn't want that; a fish soup should have a strong, distinct fish taste.

#35 One of the most popular national cuisines is Irish stew. However, it has a wide range of precise recipes, including different kinds of meats and vegetables, which are inconsistent from one location to the next and even over time.

The most frequent components are potatoes, onions, parsley, carrots, and lamb or mutton. I thought this was a wonderful hearty farmers' meal and really enjoyed it! I adore authentic cuisine as a typical Portuguese person!

#36 The last dish is the coddle, which is often cooked using leftovers and lacks a set recipe. However, layers of coarsely chopped sausages and rashers, chunky potatoes, sliced onion, bacon, salt, pepper, and herbs are usually included.

The coddle is the ultimate comfort dish, prepared in the style of a filling, healthy stew. Dublin is the greatest spot to sample it because of its strong association with the city.

#37 Ireland and the UK naturally share certain traditional foods. The Sheppard pie, fish and chips, fudge, and both black and white pudding are the most well-known. So, if you like any of these, seize the chance to sample them in Ireland.

Costs & Expenses

#38 Ireland is an expensive place to visit, as is much of Western Europe. Your budget will be impacted by the cost of lodging, food, transportation, and attractions.
On the whole, we thought Northern Ireland was a little cheaper than the Republic of Ireland.

#39 What kind of money is in use in Ireland? The Euro is the official currency of the Republic of Ireland, whereas the British Pound is used in Northern Ireland. You should be aware that you cannot utilize one currency in another nation while withdrawing money.

#40 As far as we could tell, both Northern Ireland and the Republic of Ireland accept credit and debit cards extensively, and there are no ATM fees.
However, keep in mind that your bank can impose one or more fees, and you'll likely need to withdraw money in a foreign currency.

#41 How much does a week in Ireland cost then? Without flights, we were only able to spend around 550 euros, or about 70 euros per person each day. But this number may easily be double or triple that. Nevertheless, those figures also suggest that, despite being pricey overall,

it is still feasible to make it affordable if you:

- buy at least one meal at supermarkets (we really like Centra);
- don't spend a lot of money at bars;
- travel during the shoulder or off-peak seasons;
- travel in a group (to save on lodging and transportation costs);
- and use apartments and Airbnb rather than hotels.

Transportation & Travel Tip

#42 Getting about Ireland is made simple by using a vehicle. Many of Ireland's most famous sights are spread out in rural areas, making it difficult and/or highly time-consuming to reach them via public transit.

Despite this, renting a vehicle in Ireland is not the friendliest of experiences. The price for a second driver is outrageous, and insurance is expensive. These suggestions for automobile rental in Ireland will certainly make your experience better.

#43 There are a few things to keep in mind if you want to hire a vehicle:
- Driving is done on the left side of the road in Ireland.
- Too many roads lack lights, are extremely small, and have very poor pavement.
- There are no strict speed restrictions.
- Ireland doesn't have many roadways.
- Even fewer of them are compensated, which is fantastic.

For individuals who desire the flexibility to travel independently and wish to spend less on lodging, campervanning is a fantastic alternative. This is a fantastic resource about camping in Ireland.

#44 Despite these oddities, driving around Ireland is really enjoyable, as one would anticipate. Driving the renowned routes we mentioned above (Ring of Kerry, Dingle Peninsula, and some of the passes & gaps) is among the greatest things to do in Ireland.
Ireland has virtually little traffic outside of Dublin and Cork, which is wonderful for tourists. If you're driving to Dublin and Cork, be prepared for heavy traffic and difficult parking. Parking won't be cheap and won't be available. For a day of parking in Dublin, you could have to spend as much as 30 euros.
Although anxious and agitated, Cork and Dublin drivers are hardly dangerous. The remainder of the island is rather calm and pleasant to travel through.

#45 We can't personally testify for Ireland's public transportation since we hardly ever utilize it. However, according to our research, they operate well and can transport you to the majority of locations. Keep in mind that this will need considerably more time.

Good To Know

#46 How is Ireland's internet service? shockingly poor At least there is mobile data. Particularly in rural regions, 3/4 G was always giving us trouble. Expect significant stretches of the nation to have inaccurate or incomplete data. This caught us off guard since we had better coverage in remote areas and far less developed nations.

The same data package as at home is provided if you are from the EU, which is fantastic.

Additionally, WiFi is available practically everywhere, including several tourist spots.

#47 Please be aware that many businesses, especially tourist sites, shut down quite early in Ireland. However, some restaurants also shut down the kitchen at 20 or 21... Even more significant, however, is the fact that many tourist destinations are closed all winter long! Additionally, their winter schedule is not disclosed.

Whether you're planning to travel a great distance to see an attraction, be careful to find out whether it is open and when it will shut! Or you'll have a bad surprise. Throughout winter vacation, this often occurred to us.

#48 How clean is Ireland? It mostly depends on your location. The landscape is really orderly and clean, just how we anticipated Ireland to be.

But the cities weren't the same, not even the touristy, historic ones. They were often filthy, with rubbish lining the streets and a prodigious amount of chewing gums left on the sidewalk.

#49 Type G power plugs and sockets are used in Northern Ireland, the Republic of Ireland, and the UK. Similar to the rest of Europe and the UK, the standard voltage is 230 V, and the standard frequency is 50 Hz.

#50 You can get all the information you need on this website if you're unsure if you need a visa to visit Ireland.

What immunizations are required to enter Ireland? No vaccinations are mandated or regulated for visitors entering Irish ports or airports. However, for certain individuals, some vaccinations are advised.

Accommodation

For best place to stay check out the following site;
-Booking.com
-Visitdublin.com
-Airbnb.co

Day Trips, Itineraries

Trips for a single day A 2.5-hour drive from Dublin

Howth

The charming fishing hamlet of Howth, which is just a short distance from Dublin, is one of the simplest day excursions from Dublin. You can even get to this Irish village by train!

You can absolutely reserve a guided tour at this location, particularly if you want to combine a trip to the village with a trip to Malahide Castle, but you don't have to since it's simple enough to take in the town's lovely harbor, market, and castle.

Of course, Howth's major draw is located a little beyond the hamlet itself.

Any Dublin day excursion to Howth should unquestionably include the Howth Cliff Walk and Howth Lighthouse since they are both outstanding beauties.

Cashel, Kilkenny

Kilkenny, a lovely Irish town, is all a small town should be: vibrant, laid-back, with beautiful churches, and, to top it all off, with a magnificent castle.

It's also the ideal location to visit in conjunction with Cashel for a fantastic Dublin day trip.

The fifth-century conversion of the King of Munster to Christianity is said to have taken place at The Rock of Cashel, which is located high on a rock overlooking the surrounding landscape.

Long before the Normans came to Ireland, the Rock of Cashel was also home to the kings of Munster.

At the site now, there is an outstanding collection of Celtic art, and there are breathtaking views of the landscape around.

If you're in the area, be sure to stop at Hore Abbey, which is just a short distance from Cashel and is visible from both the Rock of Cashel and Hore Abbey.

Not only are the remains of Hore Abbey breathtakingly lovely, but admission is also free!

Wicklow Mountains

On your day trip from Dublin, do you want to see the countryside? Make your way to Wicklow Mountains National Park!

This amazing national park, which is also known as "the Garden of Ireland" because of how lush it is, is also the location of an early Christian village, the remains of which you may see during your day in the Wicklow Mountains.

The Wicklow Mountains are a terrific choice for a day trip from Dublin, whether you want to take a picturesque drive, go hiking for the whole day (don't forget a raincoat!), learn about the local history, or do all of the above.

Waterford

Do you know Waterford Crystal?

If so, you at least have a general understanding of the Irish town of Waterford.

Any list of the top day excursions from Dublin should include the picturesque town of Waterford because of its magnificent harbor, great history going back to the Vikings, and the opportunity to see the Waterford Crystal Factory in the town where the business was founded.

The factory is absolutely worth seeing, whether you like costly, glittery items or not. The whole tour far surpassed our expectations and was really intriguing.

A unique activity to do in Ireland is undoubtedly taking a tour of the Waterford Crystal Factory.

Hill Of Tara

A day trip to the Hill of Tara may be the best choice for you if you're fascinated by the earliest periods of Irish history.

The hill and the buildings atop it have long been important in Irish history; the oldest still-standing structure is a burial mound from 3,000 BCE!

After a few thousand years, the Hill of Tara served as the location for the coronations of Tara's kings throughout the Iron Age and Early Christian Era, until it was finally abandoned in the 11th century.

Hook Peninsula

Although the Hook Peninsula in County Wexford is one of our favorite spots in Ireland, it may not be the most well-known of these day excursions from Dublin. However, it deserves to be on the list.

This is the excursion for you if you're seeking a day trip that is a little bit autonomous and unusual and on which you won't encounter many groups of foreign tourists.

The John F. Kennedy Arboretum, the Hook Lighthouse, Tintern Abbey, and the allegedly haunted Loftus Hall are just a few of the immensely fascinating (and beautiful!) locations that can be found on the Hook Peninsula.

Loftus Hall, which is said to be the most haunted structure in Ireland, is interesting to visit for its historical narratives, interactive ghost stories, and, surprisingly, its staircase, which is a magnificent design unique to the residence and found in just three other places on earth.

In the Pope's palace in Vatican City, the first of these stairs are located. The Titanic and the Second are both submerged underwater. And the third is right here in the Old East of Ireland.

Belfast

Even though the majority of the day excursions from Dublin described here take place in the Republic of Ireland, Belfast deviates from the norm.

Any trip to Dublin must include some time spent learning about the history of The Troubles, including the Peace Walls that physically divide the city. Belfast, the capital city of Northern Ireland, is full of fascinating sights, including plenty of (recent) history surrounding them.

Belfast's history should not, however, simply be focused on The Troubles; you should also take the time to learn about Belfast Castle, St. George's Market, and Belfast City Hall. The Titanic was constructed in Belfast.

Galway

If you want to compare Dublin to a completely different Irish city, take a day trip to the vibrant and active Galway, which is located on Ireland's west coast near where the River Corrib empties into the Atlantic Ocean.

On a day of exploration, Galway offers a variety of enjoyable activities: see the Spanish Arches, spend the afternoon in 18th-century Eyre Square, stroll down lovely Shop Street, listen to traditional Irish music in one of Galway's many renowned pubs, or even take to the water on a boat tour.

The Cliffs of Moher and Galway are also included in this wildly popular day trip from Dublin.

Day Trips from Dublin More Than 2.5 Hours Away

To emphasize that these make for very long, exhausting days and are best achieved through a scheduled trip, I purposefully isolated these three-day excursions from Dublin, Ireland—which are unquestionably among the most well-liked in the nation.

I'm not suggesting to go—believe me, I completely understand the want to visit fantasy locations whenever the chance arises, even if the circumstance is not ideal—but think twice before you go.

By doing this, issues like driving instructions, opening and closing hours, ticket purchases, lunch stops, etc. are all taken care of for you, making your vacation as stress-free as possible and enabling you to concentrate all of your attention on the breathtaking beauty!

Cliffs Of Moher

The Cliffs of Moher live up to the hype: the cliffs are genuinely incredibly beautiful, and a visit here is sure to satisfy anyone looking for stunning views in Ireland. They are probably the most well-known tourist destination in the entirety of Ireland (and unquestionably one of the most popular day trips from Dublin, despite the logistical challenges).

The Cliffs of Moher need more travel time than any of the other day excursions from Dublin on the list since they are more than three hours each way from Dublin.

That doesn't mean you shouldn't go, but it does mean that you should be ready for a very, very long day. However, if you've always wanted to visit the Cliffs of Moher, we doubt that you'll mind the effort too much once you're perched on the edge of Ireland and gazing out over the Atlantic Ocean.

One of Ireland's most well-liked and highly-rated day trips is to the Cliffs of Moher.

This one also includes time in Galway if you don't want to spend as much time at the cliffs itself!

Causeway Coast + Giant's Causeway

The seashore in Northern Ireland known as the Giant's Causeway, which is made up of 40,000 basalt columns, is second only to the Cliffs of Moher in terms of popularity among tourists.

Giant's Causeway's convenient proximity to numerous other attractions, including the Carrick-a-Rede bridge and a significant number of Game of Thrones filming locations, along with the fact that the Causeway Coast is one of the best day trips from Dublin make it clear why.

This day trip, which is 3 hours from Dublin, isn't something you should take lightly, but if you're up for the long day, experts have compiled some incredibly well-liked tours that cover a wide range of interests: this one is ideal for Game of Thrones fans like us and includes a trip to Belfast!

Cork + Blarney Castle

Achieve "the gift of the gab" by kissing the Blarney Stone at Blarney Castle in medieval times.

You may take one of the most well-liked day excursions from Dublin if three hours each way isn't too expensive to pay!

This much-liked day trip offers the option to see Blarney Castle, one of Ireland's most visited castles, as well as the gorgeous English Market in Cork, a place your taste buds will undoubtedly appreciate visiting, and a stop at the Rock of Cashel.

BONUS

20 THINGS IRELAND IS FAMOUS FOR

#1 The Emerald Island

Ireland's island and many colors of green are its initial claim to fame. The island is completely covered with grass, plants, and trees as a result of the heavy rains. It was given the moniker "Emerald Island" because of the stunning beauty of its undulating hills and lush valleys. It's interesting to note that the phrase "emerald island" first appeared in literature in the 1795 poem "When Erin First Rose" by William Drennan.

#2 St. Patrick's Day

The primary patron saint of Ireland is honored on March 17 each year, when the Irish celebrate Saint Patrick's Day. Originally a religious event, St. Patrick's Day has developed into a celebration of the whole Irish way of life, complete with parades, specialty cuisine, dancing, music, drinking, and a ton of green. Basically, it is a lot of what we shall cover here.

The national festival most widely observed is Saint Patrick's Day. It is extensively observed outside of Ireland and the UK in the US, Canada, Argentina, Australia, New Zealand, and Brazil. It is one of the things that remind us of Irish culture and was developed into a worldwide celebration by the Irish diaspora.

#3 Shamrocks

The Shamrock, a young clover with three leaves, has been one of Ireland's symbols since the 18th century. According to legend, Saint Patrick compared the three leaves of the shamrock to the Christian Holy Trinity. Shamrocks are widely present in everything Irish, including St. Patrick's Day parades.

In actuality, the shamrock represents more than just what Ireland is known for—it represents Ireland itself!

#4 Leprechauns

How has Ireland achieved fame? because it's the home of the leprechauns! The most well-known character in Irish mythology may be the leprechaun.

This supernatural character is sometimes represented as a little bearded guy with a hat and coat that are frequently green or greenish and who engages in mischief. One of the primary legends surrounding leprechauns is that they have a pot of gold hidden at the end of a rainbow. Another claim is that if you manage to catch one, you could have three wishes granted.

Leprechauns have grown to be an unofficial icon of Ireland, and you'll see lots of them during a Saint Patrick's Day parade. Even a Leprechaun museum exists in Dublin.

#5 Guinness

One of the most popular brands in the world today is Guinness, which had its origins in Dublin in 1759. This dark Irish dry stout was created at the Arthur Guinness brewery and is presently sold in 120 nations and made in 50. Although it is clearly extremely well-liked by Irish people both at home and abroad, it is also a favorite of many others, selling around 1 billion liters annually.

Malted barley and roasted malted barley are the sources of Guinness' unique flavor. It is said that aged beer was mixed with new beer to produce a sharp lactic acid flavor, although the company has not acknowledged this. The draught beer's thick, creamy head is created by adding nitrogen and carbon dioxide to the beer.

With 20 million visits since it opened in 2000, the Guinness Storehouse is another well-liked tourist attraction in Dublin.

#6 Irish whiskey

#6 Irish whiskey is a close second to Guinness as the most well-known alcoholic beverage in Ireland and worldwide. Irish whiskey used to be the most widely consumed alcoholic beverage worldwide. The industry was hurt by a protracted downturn in the 20th century, and it took until the 1990s for it to recover. Only two remained in 1967, down from over 30 in the 19th century.

Irish whiskey typically has three distillations and is smooth, warm, and a little bit sweet. Bushmills and Jameson are the two most well-known and well-liked brands. While Jameson is the whiskey that sells the most worldwide, Bushmills is the oldest legally operating whiskey distillery worldwide.

The number of distilleries has increased to over 30, and whiskey is once again one of Ireland's most well-known exports.

7 Irish Coffee

Irish coffee, for those who don't know or have never tasted it, is a hot beverage prepared with hot coffee, Irish whiskey, sugar, and cream on top. Through the cream, one should sip the coffee.

Several people have claimed to be the inventor of this drink, but Joe Sheridan, the head chef of the restaurant on the Foynes Airbase in Limerick, is the most well-known. When people were getting off the ship, he would give it to them so they could get warm. This well-liked beverage spread fast among cafes and restaurants all over the globe.

#8. Irish pubs and tar temples

I've spoken about well-known Irish drinks; now let's look at the pubs where I often consume them. Both in Ireland and abroad, Irish bars are a cultural staple. There are probably Irish pubs in every major tourist destination on the planet.

The Irish pub culture is particularly accessible since there are pubs all around Ireland, even in rural areas. We advise you to visit a small venue for a more local experience, and if you're traveling to Dublin, we advise you to visit Temple Bar to see the city's busiest tourist destination.

In addition to Irish beer, many pubs provide live music and céili dance, as well as the opportunity to try Irish food. But despite the relaxed mood, energetic and informal talks with locals are unheard of.

#9 Music

The music should be at the top of the list when determining what Ireland is most known for.

Many well-known musicians and bands from throughout the globe are from Ireland. Ireland's music scene features a wide variety of genres, from traditional folk music to rock bands. The fact that Ireland is the only nation to have won the Eurovision song contest three times is a straightforward illustration of great musical prowess.

In hindsight, it's improbable that you haven't heard some Irish music, whether it be one of the great pop-rock successes or some well-liked folk music.

#10 Riverdance

Ireland hosted the festival in 1994 after winning the competition in 1993, and during the 7-minute intermission act, one of the most impressive music and dance performances ever created, Riverdance, was presented.

This ground-breaking display of Irish dancing and music became an immediate success all over the world and quickly grew into a spectacle all on its own. The perfect blending of traditional and contemporary music, Irish dancing, and choirs captured the audience's hearts and made them fall in love with Irish culture. The program is still being presented right now.

#11 Intelligent authors

We've discussed well-known musicians, but if there's anything more amazing than all the wonderful music that comes from Ireland, it's the literary brilliance of its authors.

Ireland, which has a population of barely more than 5 million, has produced four Nobel laureates: Samuel Beckett (1969), and Seamus Heaney (1995), W. B. Yeats (1923),George Bernard Shaw (1925). Dublin is also recognized as a UNESCO City of Literature.

However, in addition to these well-regarded authors, there are many more well-known ones, such as Jonathan Swift, the author of Gulliver's Travels

In addition to numerous others, such as Bram Stoker, Roddy Doyle, Cecelia Ahern, Anne Enright, and Brendan Behan, James Joyce, the author of "Ulysses," Oscar Wilde, the author of "The Picture of Dorian Gray,"

#12 Famous Irish individuals

There are notable Irish in practically every subject, including science, the arts, and sports, therefore the list of famous Irish individuals is fairly lengthy. There are many more, but we have already covered all the well-known authors (George Bernard Shaw, Oscar Wilde, James Joyce, etc.) and artists (Bono from U2, Enya, Van Morrison, etc.).

There are a lot of Oscar nominees and A-listers on the list of actors who are Irish, including:

David Neeson

John C. Farrell

Ronan Saoirse

Connor Murphy

Frazer Brosnan

Gleeson, Brendan

Jackson Gambon

Byrne, Gabriel

There are a lot of sports on the list, but we should highlight a few.

- Conor McGregor, the featherweight and lightweight champion in mixed martial arts
- George Best, the flashy winger for Manchester United and Northern Ireland.
- Roy Keane, a former Manchester United defense midfielder;
- Pádraig Harrington is a golfer,
- Sonia O'Sullivan is a track and field athlete, and
- Brian O'Driscoll is one of rugby's all-time greats.

Other well-known Irish personalities include Michael Collins, a key role in the war for Irish independence, Mary Robinson, a former president of Ireland and High Commissioner for Human Rights for the UN, and Francis Beaufort, a scientist who created the Beaufort Scale.

#13 Red heads

The majority of people also associate Ireland with having individuals with red hair. You may be shocked to learn that just 10% of Irish people have naturally red hair if you believe that the majority of them do.

However, there is a rationale for its being one of Ireland's most well-known characteristics as it is one of the nations with the largest proportion of redheads per capita. Only Scotland has a larger proportion (13% of the population having red hair).

Only 1% to 2% of individuals worldwide have red hair, and the color may range greatly from deep burgundy to brilliant copper to burned orange and strawberry blond. Redheads are very uncommon, but if you're a fan, Scotland and Ireland are the greatest destinations to visit!

#14 Famous Landmarks

The green island is endowed with great scenic beauty and a number of well-known sites, both man-made and natural, in addition to all the amusing cultural and historical characteristics of Ireland and the Irish. The Cliffs of Moher, which attract over 1.5 million tourists a year, are perhaps the most well-known site. However, other well-known and worthwhile UNESCO heritage sites include Newgrange, the Skellig Islands, and the Giant's Causeway.

The Burren, Killarney National Park, and the Ring of Kerry are among further notable locations. A wide variety of man-made structures, like the Blarney Castle, Glendalough, the Rock of Cashel, and the Trinity College Library, are also present throughout Ireland.

#15 Book of Kells

The book of Kells is a well-known book that hasn't been included in our discussion of great authors. The Book of Kells, an illuminated composed gospel book including gospels of the New Testament and various prefatory texts and tables, is regarded as the oldest book still in existence. It was made at a Columban monastery in about 800 AD and was written in Latin.

It is regarded as a masterpiece of Western calligraphy and the apex of insular illumination. Why it is considered a sacred relic and one of

Ireland's national treasures is simple to comprehend. Two of the four volumes of the book of Kells are on exhibit at the Trinity College Library in Dublin, showing an image and a typical text page.

#16 Places for films
The beautiful splendor of Ireland has served as the setting for some of the most well-known television series and films. In fact, it's improbable that you haven't seen the green island's natural beauty and landmarks in a number of these shows:
- The amazing Star Wars (VIII and IX) Skellig Luke Skywalker takes refuge with Michael.
- Skellig Islands and the Cliffs of Moher in Harry Potter.
- Northern Ireland served as the location for various Game of Thrones filming sites.
- Saving Private Ryan
- Braveheart
- Mobby. Dick
- Normal folks were shot in Sligo since it is where most of the program is set.

#17 Among the Celtic nations
For what is Ireland renowned? To be Celtic! In reality, many of Ireland's most recognizable characteristics have Celtic roots or are connected to them. Given that it is the largest and has the most native speakers among the few Celtic countries in Europe, Ireland may also be the most well-known. Scottish, Bretton, Welsh, and Gaelic (Irish) are also regarded as Celtic languages.

#18 The Two Irelands
Ireland is well-known for being split between the Republic of Ireland and Northern Ireland, which is a component of the United Kingdom. Five-sixths of the island is occupied by the Republic of Ireland, which has a far greater population.

Simply said, the Government of Ireland Act of 1920 saw the UK divide the island into a southern region that was mostly Catholic and a northern region that was predominately Protestant. Northern Ireland is still a part of the UK, whereas the southern portion formed the Republic of Ireland.

This religious division led to several issues, including civil arrests and even acts of terrorism. Throughout the bulk of the 20th century, all of these incidents were regularly covered by the press, which greatly damaged the Irish people's reputation. Thankfully, much of it is behind us.

#19 IRA

The Irish Republican Army, a paramilitary group, aimed to liberate Northern Ireland from British authority and eventually unify Ireland as an independent republic. They were also known officially as the "Provos" and as the Provisional Irish Republican Army. Since it was the most active organization during the Troubles, the UK classified it as a terrorist group.

More than 1700 individuals were murdered during the IRA's armed campaign, including up to 300 IRA members as well as up to 1000 British military personnel and up to 650 civilians. The 1997 declaration of the last cease-fire and the inclusion of its political wing in the peace negotiations led to the 1998 Good Friday Agreement and the conclusion of the war in 2005.

As a result, for approximately 40 years, the Provisional IRA was perhaps the group most associated with Ireland and the major reason why Ireland was virtually always featured in worldwide headlines.

#20 The Great Famine

The Irish Great Famine, which lasted from 1845 to 1849, caused widespread disease and malnutrition in Ireland. The population fell by nearly 25%, from 8.4 million in 1844 to 6.6 million in 1851, as a result of around 1 million deaths and another million emigrations over these four years.

Due to emigration and decreasing birth rates, the population kept declining until it was nearly half what it had been in 1840 by the time Ireland gained independence from the UK in 1920. Ireland's population is actually lower now, 150 years after the famine, demonstrating how powerful it was.

As a result of a prolonged failure of the potato crops, this crisis is sometimes referred to as the "potato famine." Due to a late disease that kills the plant's leaves and tasty roots, this harvest failed. For a variety of economic reasons, the Irish were completely reliant on potatoes, and the UK government did nothing. Finally, it is regarded as the greatest famine that occurred in Europe throughout the 19th century.

Even if it's a very unpleasant reality, even though it isn't the major item for which Ireland is known, but it must be included in any list of interesting things about Ireland.

Made in United States
Troutdale, OR
12/09/2023

15577520R00031